Quit Smoking

Effortlessly Achieve Permanent Smoking Cessation: Embrace A Life Free From Tobacco By Implementing These Straightforward And Highly Efficient Measures

(Overcoming Nicotine Dependence: Simple Method To Quit Smoking And Enhance Quality Of Life)

Kieron Britton

TABLE OF CONTENT

Finding the Triggers 1
Why is quitting so difficult? 7
How to End An Addiction 20
Make More Time for People Who Don't Drink 39
So, How Can It Be Stopped Most Effectively? .. 83
The Difficulties of Giving Up Smoking 91
The mechanism of action of nicotine 101
Commonly Asked Queries 109

Finding the Triggers

A critical first step in comprehending your habits and actions, including smoking, is identifying your triggers. The events, feelings, or ideas that cause you to carry out a certain behavior—in this case, smoking—are known as triggers. You can create ways to control or avoid your triggers by being aware of them, which will ultimately assist you in changing your smoking behaviors for the better. Here's a comprehensive guide on recognizing smoking triggers:

Recognize Trends: Observe the trends and regularities in your smoking habits. Look for patterns in the times of day, circumstances, or events that make you want to grab a cigarette. Do you typically smoke, for instance, during breaks, after meals, or when you're stressed? Finding these trends will tell you important information about your triggers.

Emotional Intelligence: Feelings are a major factor in initiating smoking habits. Make a note of your feelings before, during, and after smoking. Stress, anxiety, boredom, irritation, and even happiness are common emotional triggers. Consider if smoking helps you deal with or get rid of these feelings.

Social Influences: Take into account the social environment in which you smoke. Consider whether you smoke more frequently in particular social circumstances or around particular persons. Social pressure, the need to fit in, or peer pressure can all be significant smoking triggers. Examine how social factors affect your smoking habits and devise plans to avoid those triggers or engage in different social activities.

Cues from the Environment: Analyze the actual settings where you frequently find yourself reaching for a smoke. Certain locations—such as particular rooms, outdoor spaces, or environments—may come to be connected with smoking. Keep an eye out for these signs and record whether being in such situations makes you feel more inclined to smoke. Understanding what triggers the environment might help you designate areas that are smoke-free or identify better activities to do there.

Habits and Rituals: Smoking frequently combines elements of other customs and habits. Determine the times of day or activities that you usually smoke. Do you, for instance, immediately light up a cigarette when you wake up, while you're driving, or when you take a break from work? These routines and behaviors have the potential to become potent stressors that lead you to smoke. You can intentionally disrupt the cycle of smoking and switch to healthy options by being aware of these associations.

Withdrawal from Nicotine: An addiction to nicotine can produce physiological cues that lead to smoking habits. When attempting to reduce your smoking or go without smoking for a while, pay attention to any physical side effects or cravings you encounter. Understand that these urges may serve as catalysts, causing you to pick up smoking once more. Navigating through and conquering these triggers will require developing ways to manage the symptoms of nicotine withdrawal.

Note and Examine: To keep track of your smoking triggers, keep a notebook or log. Note down the situations, thoughts, feelings, and circumstances that accompany smoking whenever you have the want to do so. Add information about the area, people there, time of day, and any noteworthy happenings. Over time, reviewing your diary entries on a regular basis will assist you in recognizing trends and typical triggers.

Ask for Feedback: If you smoke, you might want to ask trusted family members, friends, or support groups for their opinions. They might offer insightful views or helpful information about your triggers that you might not have thought of. Their viewpoints can aid in deepening your comprehension of your smoking patterns and triggers.

Consider Your Own Past: Examine your past experiences and personal history to find any connections or incidents that might be related to the things that make you want to smoke. For instance, your smoking behaviors may have been influenced by trauma, particular childhood situations, or big life transitions. Investigating these links can promote personal development and provide you with a better understanding of your triggers.

Why is quitting so difficult?

Reasons why quitting is difficult.

As previously mentioned in the chapter, cigarettes contain nicotine, a highly addictive substance. Your body responds to nicotine in a variety of ways, such as boosting your energy, promoting relaxation, and elevating your mood. These effects ultimately lead to addiction. Furthermore, when you haven't had cigarettes in a while, the nicotine in them makes you feel a little queasy and nauseous.

Nicotine becomes accustomed to your body and brain, so smoking cigarettes with it seems "normal." When you don't get your fix of nicotine, you start to feel withdrawal symptoms. You might find yourself wanting to smoke again just once. In fact, studies have shown that smokers simply have a tendency to meet their desires for nicotine by delivering it to their bloodstream at the appropriate moment. Your body and mind become upset if you don't accomplish this. Your entire being begs you to continue smoking. You feel more uncomfortable and agitated the less you smoke. The need to eat or have sex is not as intense as the want to smoke in order to feel "normal" again. See why it's so difficult to give up smoking?

When it comes to managing the symptoms of nicotine withdrawal, most people fail to stop smoking before they even begin. The fact that smoking has become a daily practice is another important factor contributing to the difficulty of quitting. You get used to lighting up and puffing on cigarettes every day. These "relaxing" smoking breaks become something you look forward to. Whether you smoke in your car, read the newspaper, or simply hang out with friends, breaking this habit becomes incredibly difficult since it becomes ingrained in who you are and how you live your life.

Making the intentional decision to stop smoking and using the appropriate tools to help break the habit and nicotine addiction are the most important aspects of quitting.

Variations in the Make-Up of Skin Tissue

Smoking can cause quick alterations in the tissues that make up the skin. According to a study, smokers had a higher chance of developing elastosis, a disorder where the skin's connective tissues rapidly deteriorate and lose their flexibility.

Experts were also able to confirm that smokers have more elastosis and that it is more severe than nonsmokers'elastosis by computer-assisted study.

Furthermore, smokers have an increased risk of developing telangiectasia. Fine red lines, which result from the skin's tiny blood vessels dilating, are the hallmark of this illness.

Smoking more cigarettes per day raises the risk of developing telangiectasia or elastosis.

Is the damage to your lungs irreversible, or can they recover after smoking?

A team of medical professionals created WebMD.com to give anybody with an Internet connection access to health and wellness information. They don't hold back when discussing the fatal risks associated with smoking.

The free, internationally renowned online health advocate claims that "smoking's damage is swift and irreversible." There are extensive consequences, just like with many lifestyle decisions.

Researchers in the United States and other countries started to realize the very real and extremely long-lasting harm that smoking does to the body and mind in the 1970s and 1980s. Did you know, for example, that...

A single cigarette stiffens the arteries by 25% in a young individual starting to smoke, even if they have never been around secondhand smoke. This increases cardiac workload.

That may not even be the whole extent of the damage. As American researcher Stella Daskalopoulou, MD, notes, "...cigarette smoking starts inflicting very significant damage on the arteries with the very first puffs taken by otherwise healthy young smokers." Smoking tobacco products puts a lot of pressure and stress on the lungs in addition to the heart.

Cigarette smoking is the cause of between 75% and over 90% of lung cancer cases, no matter where people smoke. This raises the question of whether lung damage from smoking may be repaired or if it is a lifelong condition.

Some Smoking-Related Lung Damage Is Irreversible and Permanent

The unfortunate reality is that smoking even a small amount damages the lungs over time. This is not to argue that if you smoke currently, you shouldn't stop right away because if you stop smoking tobacco products, your body will start to heal significantly in regions such as the lungs and other departments.

Tobacco smoke is particularly effective in eliminating cilia, which are a natural defense mechanism in your lungs.

Any working cilia will revert to their naturally healthy functions as soon as you quit smoking. But the cilia you've destroyed are irreversibly damaged and cannot grow again. Furthermore, smoking causes long-term harm to the lung's air sacs, which increases the chance of developing Chronic Obstructive Pulmonary Diseases (COPD), which include emphysema and chronic bronchitis.

Your heart, lungs, and overall body suffer greater harm the more you smoke. No organ in your body is immune to the damaging effects of tobacco smoke. Make every effort to give up smoking right now.

Research indicates that even if you have smoked heavily in the past, your chance of getting lung cancer is the same 10 to 15 years after you stop smoking as it is for someone who has never smoked.

Just keep in mind that every puff you inhale causes irreversible lung damage, which you cannot reverse—you can only avoid it.

What Perils Come With Idle Smoking?

Do you have any smoking friends? If so, you might be dying at their hands. You should take passive smoking seriously if you spend time in a smoking environment. Passive smoking is also known as secondhand smoke (SHS) or environmental tobacco smoke (ETS).

In many nations these days, smoking is prohibited in restaurants and other public areas by legislation. This has significantly decreased the risk of secondhand smoke exposure for nonsmokers. You are exposed to the chemicals in the smoke if you enter a room where there isn't any obvious smoke because the chemicals have seeped into the carpet, flooring, draperies, furniture, and the physical environment of that space from frequent smokers.

The smoke from passive smoking can harm you just as much as that of "active" or intended smokers, aside from possibly causing you a headache and leaving a terrible odor on your clothing. Exposure to secondhand tobacco smoke, even on rare occasions, can result in illness, disability, and even death.

Elements of addiction that are psychological.

How to locate and make use of assistance

Here are some methods for locating and utilizing assistance to overcome addiction:

Investigation: Find out which forms of help—such as counseling or support groups—might be most effective for you by researching your alternatives.

Speak up: Never hesitate to get in touch with various support channels if you have any questions or need further details. To find out more about a support group's or therapist's services, for instance, give them a call.

Attend Meetings: To network with other individuals undergoing recovery and to gain further insight into the process, attend therapy sessions or support group meetings.

Request for Suggestions: Consult your physician, therapist, or other medical professionals for recommendations on supportive services that could be beneficial to you.

Link Up Online: For individuals in recovery, a plethora of online services are accessible, including forums and online support groups. Use these resources to establish connections with other people.

Use Helplines: A lot of organizations have helplines where those who are battling addiction can get assistance and direction. These hotlines can be a very useful tool for receiving prompt assistance and direction.

But having a network of support can be quite beneficial. One cannot stress how crucial support is to beating addiction. Help offers a feeling of responsibility, comprehension, practical and emotional support, and inspiration to carry on with the healing process.

There are numerous choices available for locating and obtaining help, such as peer support, online resources, family and friends, sober living, therapy, and support groups. Finding the best kind of support for you may need some study, contacting various support sources, attending meetings, getting recommendations, interacting online, and calling helplines.

Recall that getting support and assistance during your recuperation is not a sign of weakness. In actuality, asking for assistance requires bravery. You may effectively traverse the difficulties of recovery and attain long-term sobriety if you have the correct support network in place.

How to End An Addiction

How, then, do you approach it? Creating a plan should be your first action. A plan puts things in motion and helps to make quitting a practical, achievable, and feasible process.

You must specify your smoking habits, including what kind of smoker you are, why you smoke, and when you smoke when creating the plan. Selecting a plan that best suits your needs is made simple when all these areas are identified.

Do you smoke a pack a day? Are you over a pack-a-day smoker? Are you the only one who smokes when it's appropriate in social situations? Do you smoke for addiction? Consider which issue I choose to resolve with cigarettes. When you're anxious or depressed, do you smoke? Or perhaps just to go for a quick break with intriguing people? Be truthful with yourself, jot down the reasons, and then consider how you can make decisions without smoking. It's easier to follow the optimal plan if you know the answers to these questions.

The following should be part of your smoking plan:

Maybe there are important, important factors behind this. For instance, having the capacity to endure a stressful workday. Talk about things you can't talk in the office in the smoking room.

Speak with your loved one over the phone. Join a group of intriguing people or make new friends. The gap in your lifestyle is obvious when you give up smoking on the same day. Holding a cup of coffee, however, there's a missing piece. And all the enjoyment is ruined by this deficiency. Put another way, a smoke break used to be a very legal method to take a break, but since you stopped smoking, it doesn't seem like there's any need for one nowadays. Thus, you keep working nonstop, wearing down your neurological system and putting yourself into a chronic condition of exhaustion. Your subconscious mind's attempt to return a cigarette that is connected with joy and relaxation is not uncommon. And trust me, it will come back!

As a result, you must select a date. Not too distant to avoid changing your mind, nor too close to ensure that you are prepared.

The following are part of the preparation. You must break the link between smoking and pleasure in daily life. If you often like your cup of coffee with a cigarette, try this instead. Make a self-promise to yourself, such as, "I will smoke in 15 minutes and drink coffee now," and follow through on it. If you must engage in casual conversation with coworkers, do it without smoking while reminding yourself that you will take a vacation from smoking later.

When day X finally arrives, you will already be psychologically prepared, so it won't be as difficult.

Have a deadline: Without a deadline, a plan would just keep running without getting anything done. Setting a date for your quit helps you stay motivated to see it through. Select a date within a specific time range, such as two weeks or twelve days. You are now sufficiently motivated to give up smoking.

Inform people of your intention to stop the habit, and they will provide you with support and encouragement to help you get through it. Relatives, friends, or loved ones can also support someone in giving up smoking.

Their encouragement and support get you through the difficult moments. Perhaps to link social media platforms as well. Although it may sound absurd, smokers who share their strategies for kicking harmful habits on social media are actually quite successful. The likelihood of using Facebook and Twitter to help you overcome your addiction to cigarettes is far higher than that of attempting to resist cigarette urges in person.

You appear to be receiving encouragement from others, perhaps because of Facebook or Twitter. Furthermore, there are a ton of inspirational tales of people who have already started smoking on social media. Furthermore, our confidence in our own triumph grows as we learn more about the triumphant experiences of others.

Get ready for the worst: the first three months will be the most difficult for you due to intense cravings for cigarettes and withdrawal from nicotine, which will make the process intolerable and drive you to relapse into smoking.

Trash all cigarettes and tobacco items. It's said that what's out of sight is out of memory. Eliminating any traces of tobacco and cigarettes increases your chances of successfully quitting. To get rid of any traces and odors of smoke, thoroughly clean your home, car, clothes, office, and surrounding areas.

Speak with your doctor about it: By discussing your plans to stop smoking with your physician, you can receive the necessary medical assistance. Certain drugs that aid with nicotine withdrawal and cigarette cravings can be prescribed by your doctor. During this time, gums, lozenges, and nicotine patches are also quite beneficial.

Find out what causes your desires by keeping a journal of them. This can help you identify patterns in your cravings and identify their triggers. Note how long the need lasted, how strong it was, and how you felt both before and after smoking.

Explore for an alternative – The best course of action is to explore alternative ways to relieve stress, as smoking is typically a result of depressive or stressful situations. There are effective alternative approaches for quitting smoking, such as breathing exercises, exercise, relaxation techniques, and meditation.

While they could feel like your sole buddy on hectic days, cigarettes are actually your deadliest enemy.

Determining the social and emotional factors that affect addictive behavior

Addiction-related behaviors can be impacted by a variety of social and emotional factors. Comprehending these constituents is crucial in formulating efficacious initiatives for the prevention and treatment of addiction. Important emotional and social factors that can fuel addictive behaviors include the following:

Emotional anguish: worry, despair, or trauma. Because addiction provides temporary comfort or an escape from these uncomfortable emotions, it can lead to a vicious cycle of dependence.

Low self-esteem: Individuals who struggle with self-worth may turn to addictive behaviors as a way to boost their confidence or fit in with a particular social group. Substance abuse or addictive behaviors might provide a brief sense of worth or validation. Peer pressure: Social variables have a significant impact on addiction. Peer pressure can cause people to experiment with addictive substances or engage in obsessive behaviors in an attempt to fit in or avoid social isolation. The desire to fit in or adhere to

Family and social context: Adopting addictive behaviors might be made more likely by having family members who are addicts or by growing up in an environment where addiction is prevalent. Emotional distress and the risk of addiction can also result from abuse, neglect, or a lack of social support. A further component is dysfunctional family dynamics.

Addiction can be significantly impacted by the accessibility of drugs or behaviors that are addictive. Easy access to drugs, alcohol, gambling, and other addictive activities may make it simpler for people to engage in and develop dependence on addictive behaviors.

Impact of the press: People's perceptions of addictive substances or behaviors might be influenced by media portrayals and social norms. Media, such as TV shows, movies, ads, and social media, can normalize or glamorize addictive behaviors.

People who use drugs or other addictive behaviors to self-medicate or ease their symptoms of anxiety, depression, PTSD, or attention-deficit/hyperactivity disorder (ADHD) may develop addictive behaviors as a result of these conditions.

The Swedish approach

To begin with, "The Swedish method" does not exist. In Sweden, there's only one thing that's popular. However, it wouldn't exactly be lyrical to title it "Something that is popular in Sweden," would it? What, then, do people from Sweden do? They don't smoke, yet they nevertheless ingest a lot of tobacco. Instead, they utilize "snus," which is tobacco applied beneath the upper lip for a longer amount of time.

Restrictions

Notwithstanding the fact that snus lowers the incidence of lung cancer, it is still an addiction. It is still a tobacco-related way of living, requiring a significant amount of time and effort to try to get the nicotine into the body. Additionally, speaking while wearing snus beneath the lip is quite difficult because it changes flavor and turns saliva black. Gross!

Self-doubt

Certainly not an official smoking cessation method, but one that a lot of smokers attempt. What does self-doubt look like? Actually, it's very easy. It includes reading health-related data and viewing images or films that illustrate the potential harm that smoking may have to one's health. Seeing and reading about all the horrible ways that people can pass away or suffer can serve as a powerful incentive to quit.

Restrictions

It's surprisingly not very effective. Few smokers are truly motivated to give up by knowledge of the potential harms of smoking. It is related to human nature in some way. Taking certain actions, even if one is fully aware that they could have disastrous consequences. After all, we do kill one another in conflicts, pollute the sole planet in our region of the cosmos that is habitable, and believe that we are unbreakable.

One final observation about popular smoke-cessation techniques

The most crucial thing to remember about smoking cessation techniques is that some of them genuinely do work wonders for certain individuals, so it's always worth giving them a shot.

However, your best option might be to read the following section of this book if you have already tried them and they haven't worked or if you don't want to attempt them because they are too time-consuming, too expensive, too painful, too risky, or too demanding on the body. The section describes how to stop smoking without actually stopping. Cheers!

It's Time to Give Up Smoking by Continuing to Smoke

There are three components to the approach. Or in three stages. Or three conditions that must be met, if you will, for it to function. We can also refer to these three elements as the three pillars of smoking cessation to make it seem really grandiose—even though, as we all know by now, quitting is not a one-and-done proposition.

The goal of stopping smoking without really stopping

There are two types of smoking, as we have stated in the book's introduction. Smoking is both a behavior and an act that involves breathing in and out of tobacco smoke. Only the second type of smoking—smoking as a way of life—is eligible for the goal of quitting without really stopping.

The method's goal is to keep smoking from taking over a significant portion of a person's life while still permitting the occasional indulgence. Fun is, after all, what life's all about.

The approach

Returning to the trio of splendid pillars. The first is the sincere desire. The second is the shock buffer. The third is the absence of finality.

By having a sincere desire, an elastic band, and an absence of closure, you can overcome your smoking issue. And voilà! That concludes it. Thank you for reading the book, and best of luck.

I'm kidding! You know, one of the key elements in overcoming your situation is also having a good mindset. The true desire is, in fact, a major component of the first pillar (step, component, prerequisite, etc.). It could be helpful to understand why we smoke in the first place, though, before we feel the need to quit.

What initially motivates people to smoke?

Hard to say. Not sure. What makes you smoke?

Smoking is a coping mechanism for the outside world. In the same way as writing, dancing, traveling, or drinking are. It's a personal decision that is, of course, greatly influenced by other contextual circumstances. People smoke for a variety of reasons. Every smoker has a different meaning when it comes to smoking, in the same way that dancing or writing does.

Nonetheless, there are a few widely accepted justifications for smoking.

My goal is to blend in.

It sounds absurd, doesn't it? Still, a lot of us smoke for this very frequent reason. It is evident from looking at age-related smoking statistics that smoking most frequently begins in adolescence. Our goal is to blend in with our classmates. Like them, we want to be cool. We aspire to emulate the smoking habits of our parents, grandparents, uncles, fathers, and other close relatives.

We take up smoking only to be accepted. After that, it turns into an addiction and a habit. And before we know it, we're smoking two packs a day, sneaking out of the office to sneak a cigarette, lighting it with unsteady hands whenever we get the chance, spending absurd sums of money on our unhealthy addiction, and planning our schedules so that there's always time and space for smoking. A substantial amount.

A method for reducing tension

Many smokers may tell you that they smoke because it helps them cope with stress. They also have total honesty.

They have conditioned themselves to believe that smoking helps them cope with stress. To relieve some of the tension, they may easily eat a banana, scream, or perform a few push-ups.

Smoking has become associated with stress relief on a global scale. A phenomenon shared by numerous societies and cultures. In fact, we think smoking helps reduce stress. Although there are other, far more enjoyable ways to relieve stress, the fact has already been alluded to previously.

A routine

Some smokers may merely respond that they genuinely don't know why they smoke when questioned. They simply carry it out. It's a routine. Similar to buckle up in an automobile or checking the time every few minutes. It is unconsciously done.

Smokers choose to have a cigarette every time they have five seconds to consider their next move. Why? That is what happens when someone acts out of habit; they act without even having a true conscious reason for doing so. It's just a clear decision. Constantly present. Always willing to lend a helping hand.

Make More Time for People Who Don't Drink

Building strong, wholesome relationships is essential.

Being sober involves more than just staying away from your former friends who abuse drugs or alcohol. Developing new, healthy relationships and friendships with people who can and will support you in abstaining from alcohol is even more crucial.

It could seem hard to do this at first. It can seem like everyone who is normal and "has a life" drinks when you are around people who make alcohol a big part of their lives. It's not true, as stated.

Numerous individuals abstain from alcohol and actively seek out non-drinking buddies. Exactly as they are searching for others exactly like you; all you have to do is look for them. To meet sober people, you might have to try new things. Here are a few instances:

Taking part in a volunteer organization

Attend events where alcohol isn't served.

Interacting with social media groups dedicated to those who practice sobriety

As you get to know them, you'll discover that they have a variety of non-alcoholic pastimes, like fishing, hiking, skiing, and gaming. You might even find that you enjoy these pursuits far more than ones that involve drinking.

In any case, make time to interact with people who abstain from drinking. Even when you invite some men to events that are miles away from bars, they will still insist on hoarding the bottle. When they go hiking or to the theater, they'll "brown-bag" a flask.

If abstaining from alcohol is something you're genuinely devoted to, establish plans with other people who share your commitment. In this manner, you won't have to worry about the possibility of accidentally drinking alcohol when you want to relax and have fun.

It could be necessary to shut off people from your life entirely, which could be difficult, particularly if you actually enjoy them. But if you don't do this, you run the risk of never really succeeding in your fight against alcohol. It's not a friendship anymore if it works against you, is it?

Get better at saying "no" without embarrassing yourself while attempting to justify your decision to abstain from alcohol. You'll find that when you don't give in to their demands and instead stick to your principles, people—especially your friends—respect you more.

You also need to stay away from harmful connections. Many people are unable to completely give up alcohol because they are involved in numerous toxic relationships that constantly encourage them to reach for the bottle.

It won't help you avoid consuming alcohol, for instance, if your spouse constantly takes advantage of your emotions and vulnerabilities or makes you feel anxious or tense all the time.

If you're like most people who battle addiction, you've surely reached a point where your primary relationship is with the drug of your choice (in this case, alcohol). As your alcoholism worsened, your range of behaviors decreased, and you focused more of your time and energy on alcohol-related behaviors.

It's highly likely that the friends you still have are the ones you drank with or relied on to obtain your dose. In order to maintain your recovery, you may (and will) suffer great harm from relationships with past lovers and acquaintances.

you'll eventually get a haircut." This suggests that you will eventually fall back into your previous routines if you continue to associate with the same people.

Exercise is covered in the next step, which is another fundamental building piece that will inspire you and keep you away from alcoholics.

3: Individual Assistance

One of the most crucial things you can ask for from your friends and family when attempting to kick a habit as hard as smoking is moral support. We'll only cover a few of the numerous ways in which your family can support you.

Verify Their Awareness

Make sure your friends and family are aware of how difficult it can be to break a habit like smoking, especially if many of them have never tried to quit or have never smoked before. You are about to set off on a journey that is said to be addicting since it is not an easy one. Of course, some people find it easier than others, and you may find it simple to stop smoking. It could, however, be really challenging for certain individuals. Therefore, you need to ensure that they are aware of your expectations, how the experience will make you feel, and what they can do to ease your burden.

You ought to explain to them why it is so difficult as well. Make sure you discuss topics like whether or not smoking is a coping method for you with your friends and family. Following your quitting smoking, you may relapse when managing stress. This is particularly true if you are dealing with your stress on your own. Make careful to warn your family members, or consider seeking counseling.

Making sure they are aware of the strategies you want to employ in your attempt to stop is another action you can take. In this manner, they can assist you with it!

In relation to lending a hand,

Telling your friends and family that you are trying to stop smoking could also be beneficial, as they can offer you some tough love or support if you are headed for a relapse. Administering firm support is crucial when it comes to quitting smoking. Tough love can help you achieve a lot of things you may discover!

Retain Them Updated

If you believe that your family members' opinions and assistance will be beneficial, make sure they understand how much you value and even encourage their contributions. The most crucial thing you could possibly ask of your friends and family during a time like this is their active participation in the actual process of quitting.

This could entail sharing with them any cravings or emotions you are going through, even if they don't seem like big issues. Make sure you give them an opportunity to share their thoughts with you and that you grant them some degree of control over what is happening to you. This could be of great assistance, particularly when deciding whether or not to quit.

Aids for Quitting

It may be particularly tough at first when you are first starting to quit. Getting some quitting aids would be a great idea, no doubt about it. On the other hand, these could eventually become costly. Therefore, be honest with your family when they ask what they can do to help: "It would be great to have a box of patches," or "Maybe a pack of nicotine gum."

Even though the aids don't have to be extremely costly, every little bit helps! You might ask for a few packs of patches, gum, or even a new e-cigarette if you intend to quit after Christmas for your well-known New Year's Resolution. So just remember that.

The herbal pills do not, however, address the other withdrawal symptoms associated with quitting smoking cigarettes, which is a more serious issue. These are serious issues, which may be one reason why a herbal stop-smoking medication won't work.

Prescription pills are an additional type of pill. To obtain this type of medication, you should consult your family physician. These days, the market is home to a few excellent ones.

Usually, taking these pills for three to four months will be enough to help you successfully quit smoking. Not only do they address the dependence on nicotine, but they also help to alleviate the anxieties that need to be addressed regarding the withdrawal symptoms associated with quitting smoking.

One disadvantage of prescription stop-smoking pills is that not all smokers who want to quit will have access to a doctor or medical insurance to write a prescription for them.

This could be an incredibly expensive way to stop smoking cigarettes because not all insurance companies will cover the cost of the pills themselves. Some people might even believe that buying a pack of cigarettes is less expensive than giving up smoking.

If you want to use this method, you should contact your health insurance company to see if they will help with the cost of the medication by offering a co-pay.

Given the significantly higher costs an insurance company would incur should you develop cancer, some may use this as a deterrent.

There is no evidence that Chantix may cause suicidal thoughts, attempts, and blackouts.

IS A STOP SMOKING PLAN NEEDED?

Instead of worrying about the hypothetical, make plans for the inevitable!

Making a plan to stop smoking is a great way to get ready to stop. Making preparations in advance is essential to effectively stopping smoking. Planned quitting helps most people stay motivated, focused, and self-assured.

Decide when to stop.

It's best to decide on a quit date as soon as possible. Select a time slot from the upcoming two weeks. This will provide you enough time to get ready without making you want to give up.

A night out with friends or a day when you might smoke at work are examples of days when you should avoid picking.

Give up smoking on the weekend if you smoke primarily at work, so you have a few days to get used to the change.

Put a note of your quit date somewhere you can see it every day, or mark it on your calendar. This will serve as a reminder of your decision to give up smoking and provide you with enough time to get ready to stop. On your phone, you can also set a reminder.

I want to quit, but should I tell my friends, family, and coworkers?

Getting support from significant others in your life can make quitting smoking easier. Share with your loved ones your intention to give up smoking and let them know you need their help and encouragement to do so.

Determine who is available to assist you in times of need. Seek out a quit partner who is also interested in quitting smoking. You can support one another during difficult times.

However, some smokers would rather keep their decision to stay a secret from others. To prevent putting undue pressure on themselves, they keep it a secret. If they make a mistake, they believe that they have let their friends or family down. There will be less pressure on them to live up to the expectations of friends and family if they choose not to disclose.

Your choice to inform loved ones about your decision to stop smoking is perfectly acceptable. Everything is based on what's best for you.

Recognize and prepare for the obstacles you'll encounter during your quit.

The first three months following quitting are when most relapses happen. By anticipating and preparing for common challenges like nicotine withdrawal and cigarette cravings, you can better support yourself during difficult times.

Take out the tobacco products and cigarettes from your car, house, and place of employment.

Take out all visual cues related to smoking from your home, workplace, and car. Get rid of everything that might be connected to smoking, including matches, ashtrays, and lighters. It would be much easier to just take the reminders down rather than forcing yourself to fight the urge to smoke.

Donate or discard any leftover cigarettes (please, no emergency smokes!). You run a considerable risk of picking one up if you keep a pack of cigarettes in your house or place of business. This particular cigarette has the potential to hook you once more.

Clean your clothing and deodorize anything that has a cigarette odor. Vacuum your carpet and drapes, steam clean your furniture, and shampoo your car.

Consult your physician about quitting support.

In addition to offering other options, your doctor may recommend medication to aid in the withdrawal process. The nicotine patch, gum, and other over-the-counter products are available at your neighborhood pharmacy or grocery store if you are unable to see a doctor.

THE COST OF SMOKING

Forget for a minute how much your addiction to cigarettes is costing your health (shudder). Many of today's addicts, in my opinion, cannot afford to smoke.

However, have you calculated the financial toll that your cigarette addiction is taking on you and/or your family? Sincerely, have you taken a seat and completed the maths? You must. Repeat the action if you have already done it.

Your addiction will cost you more than $5,000 annually if you smoke five packs a day!

You can lose out on almost $55,000 in your savings account after ten years if you don't give up smoking and stick to your meager one-pack-a-day addiction after this first year! I am using that 'modest' $55K balance cautiously.

Remember that the price of smokes will increase up, and instead of using the low-interest savings account I mentioned, you could have invested in higher-paying CDs. In actuality, though, you could have used that money to purchase a modest condo or maybe pay off your mortgage more quickly. In a mere decade!

That dream truly vanishes in puffs of smoke if you keep smoking.

Like I did, you may have been thinking for years, "I work; I should spend my money however I wish." It is accurate. However, did you account for the cost of upcoming medical bills? Do you have adequate insurance to pay for all of the unavoidable medical costs? Do you possess disability insurance? What about long-term care insurance? Life assurance?

The cost of your deductible alone might go into the hundreds of dollars for only one week in the hospital (without surgery). Add to that oxygen therapy, equipment, job loss, transportation to and from medical facilities, medication, and carers. The list seems to go on forever.

You probably already know how much smoking costs you and your family, but keep in mind the additional costs as well. Another option is to make a list of the annual treats you and your family will receive from your savings after you stop smoking.

Putting Allies in Your Corner to Build a Robust Support System

Having a solid support network is crucial for success while starting the process of quitting smoking. Having people around you who support you, understand your objectives, and can help you in real-world situations can greatly increase your resilience and motivation. Having a strong support system means that you will always have allies who are willing to lend you the emotional and practical support you need when things get tough. Let's examine the value of having a solid support network and practical methods for creating one.

Friends and Family

Inform your close friends and family that you have decided to give up smoking. Their comprehension, motivation, and unwavering assistance are priceless. Tell them why you're quitting, what obstacles you may face, and how they can support you when things get tough. Open communication with loved ones helps you develop empathy and fortifies the ties that will keep you going on your trip.

Programs and Support Groups for Quitting Smoking

Enroll in a support group or program to help you stop smoking. These controlled settings offer a group of people with comparable objectives and backgrounds. Engaging with those who are experiencing comparable difficulties facilitates the exchange of insights, counsel, and motivation. These support groups frequently include information on resources, coping mechanisms, and techniques for successfully ending tobacco use.

Medical Experts

Talk to medical professionals who specialize in helping people quit smoking. They can monitor your progress, give medicine or nicotine replacement therapy, and provide expert guidance. Having routine check-ins with a healthcare provider can provide you with a sense of responsibility and give you access to guidance that is specifically customized for your requirements.

Internet-Based Support Groups

Investigate websites and discussion boards devoted to quitting smoking. Making connections with people who have successfully quit or are currently quitting can be incredibly beneficial in terms of information, support, and inspiration. Online groups offer a handy setting for exchanging experiences, getting counsel, and finding comfort in trying times.

Partners in Accountability

Choose a dependable friend, relative, or coworker to act as your accountability partner. This person can hold you accountable for your commitment to stopping smoking, motivate you, and help you stay on course. Frequent check-ins, progress reports, and honest dialogue with your accountability partner instill accountability and bolster your will to succeed.

Expert Guidance

For the purpose of addressing any underlying emotional or psychological issues associated with smoking, think about obtaining professional counseling or therapy. Creating healthy coping strategies, and offering continuous support as you work towards stopping.

Take Part in Healthful Activities

Engage in pastimes and pursuits that complement your smoke-free way of living. Participate in fitness programs, leisure clubs, or neighborhood associations that support healthful lifestyles. Not only may good and enjoyable activities divert your attention from smoking, but they also introduce you to like-minded people who will encourage you on your journey.

Express Your Needs

Be upfront and explicit with your support network about your needs and boundaries. Tell them how they can help you the most, if that means not smoking in your presence, providing support, or just being a listening ear. Good communication guarantees that people in your support network are aware of your objectives and are able to offer you the assistance you need.

When looking for people who will support you in your efforts to give up smoking, exercise patience and initiative. Appreciate the folks who stand by you no matter what, and show them your thanks and progress reports in return. Creating a strong support system for yourself is an investment in your healTogether, you can conquer obstacles and rejoice in the life-changing potential of quitting smoking.

How I Gave Up

Previously, I had usually given up when I became so ill that smoking only made matters worse. That is the most straightforward method for giving up smoking. Thus, in the event that you are sufficiently desperate and doubt your ability to give up on yourself. Get out there and get ill. Sit next to someone who appears to be suffering from a cold or other viral illness. Rub your eye and touch whatever they touched most recently. Being ill is the easiest approach to stop smoking there is.

I'm hoping that by sharing my own experience of quitting cold turkey with you, you'll have a different outlook on the process and be empowered to stop on your own. Gum, patches, or any type of medication are not necessary for quitting. Because of their terrible negative effects, I have never used any of these. The simplest and most straightforward way to stop smoking is what I do. You are no longer forced to live as a nicotine slave. You can accomplish it, too, if I can.

My intention was to spend the first day of my smoking cessation indoors doing activities I enjoyed. I didn't get out of bed in the morning or get a cup of coffee. They were both things that made me want to smoke. Rather, I consumed a great deal of food, watched films, and used a variety of iPhone apps.

I found that writing things down was really helpful. For me, this made everything more visible. It was more than simply a thought or a fleeting moment. Now, it was on a sheet of paper. This helps you grasp everything you need to know to stop smoking and helps you make things more clear.

Day 2 was the same, despite having an extra day off from work. I was concerned that I would not be lured into taking a cigarette. Make the choice to avoid triggers more on particular days if your schedule permits you to do so. Making things simpler for yourself is a strategy to have less stressful days rather than cheating.

I opted to stay indoors for the first two days of smoking because my schedule permitted it. I was not going to expose myself to temptation. These cravings might have caused me to light up another cigarette. And I wasn't going to allow it to occur.

The third day was difficult; I started to crave things and was strongly inclined to just resume smoking at work. I managed my urges and remained strong by keeping myself busy all the time. I was aware that if I had a few minutes to kill without getting anything done, I would probably start smoking again. This is when having a list of coping mechanisms really helped. I would select one item from the list and head to my fridge.

More than any other form of exercise, riding a bike did the trick for me. Every day, I would ride my bike farther and farther. This was a fantastic method for me to push myself. Making it up a high hill that makes you feel afraid made me feel really proud of myself and gave me the impression that I could accomplish anything.

To achieve a smoke-free month or longer, I avoided going to pubs, clubs, and other public gathering places where a large number of people were drinking. Before going a month without smoking, if I had a few beers, I would probably go buy a pack or steal one from someone.

Not only is alcohol a major trigger Being drunk increases your susceptibility to temptation. I had to learn to say no if I wanted to stay away from this kind of vulnerability. I would always say no to friends who offered to buy me a beer. I even declined an invitation to a home party. I was adamant that I would not return this time, and I did not. While there were moments when my pals were angry with me, they also knew who was and wasn't smoking. I refused to let a good time in the town wreck my future self.

Prohibited for the upcoming generation

Restricting minors' access to tobacco goods is one of the main regulating tags in the multilayered strategy to minimize tobacco consumption.

● Age verification will be necessary to prevent teenagers or students from purchasing cigarettes or other tobacco products. Individual self-care Tobacco displays were taken down because they made it easier for children to purchase or steal tobacco products.

Proper enforcement of the law has been shamefully disregarded, leading to a plethora of malpractices that have been eroding the fragile saplings even before the states have started to implement their stringent measures to keep minors away. Retailer education, compliance inspections, and enforcement actions have become the focus for sts and ● localities. Cigarette vending machines are prohibited in most states, with the exception of those where children cannot access them.

● The goals of federal policy require that all States revoke licenses for access laws that impact the primary tactic used to try to stop minors from purchasing tobacco products. The social networks that young people use, such as their friends, siblings, and parents, to purchase cigarettes must be the main emphasis of their campaign.

Teenagers' perceptions of the following elements increase their likelihood of smoking tobacco:

1. Tobacco use is the norm because their siblings and peers support them in using tobacco products.

2. The unwavering conviction that it greatly enhances mental clarity, which boosts morale in tough conditions.

3. The health dangers linked with using chewing tobacco are usually too complex for developing brains to understand.

The positive aspect

A combined anti-tobacco campaign and higher tobacco product taxes have resulted in a sharp decline in the number of smokers.

Massachusetts and California had lower rates of cigarette smokers than other US states.

The Minnesota Heart Health Programme observed a forty percent decrease in the number of community smokers at various formal events. The primary objective of this quit-smoking program was also a combined school-based curriculum. A preliminary assessment from the American Stop Smoking Intervention Study (ASSIST) later revealed a 7% decrease in the number of smokers in each of the 17 ASSIST States. Cigarette advertising and promotions should be banned in order to make tobacco products less alluring to youth. Additionally, pro-tobacco messaging should be vigorously rebutted in order to quickly and effectively reach sizable segments of the population.

The most successful ways to stop tobacco usage are, by far, those that involve television, radio, and other mass media.

Radio, magazines, and other media are used to reach broad, targeted audiences with information and educational messages; to boost public support for tobacco control policies and programs; to reinforce social norms that encourage abstinence from tobacco use; and to counteract the pro-use messaging and imagery of tobacco marketing and public relations campaigns.

Reducing the attraction of smoking

Reversing the current societal tendency that condones tobacco use is necessary to lessen the appeal of tobacco to youth. To bring about this change, we must oppose the billion-dollar cigarette promotion and advertising campaigns that mislead young, sensitive brains about tobacco use. Counter-advertising campaigns have been funded by Arizona, California, and Massachusetts in an attempt to remove such exaggerated tobacco usage appeals and draw attention to the existing risks.

Enclosed in the sheath of a puff inhaled. They were successful in informing young people about the harmful effects of tobacco use on their appearance, performance, and health. Preliminary data indicates that the media efforts have reached the youth, adults, and multicultural populations in those States, and they have been successful in achieving their objectives.

Over the past few years, advances in technology have accepted that there is no such thing as a "safe cigarette."

Reducing the nicotine and tar content of tobacco products, as well as adjusting the proportions of tobacco-specific compounds and nitrosamines used in other tobacco products, are among the issues that have been brought up and debated.

Cigarette prices increase in response to decreases in cigarette demand. The rate of smoking and chewing tobacco among adults and children increases when the excise charge on tobacco goods is increased.

For every 10% increase in cigarette prices, adult smoking rates decrease drastically by 4%.

Because teen smoking rates are more sensitive to price, there is a 7.6–12% decrease in smoking rates for every 10% increase in cigarette pricing.

APPLYING BRAIN

A mental component is involved in the act of quitting. You must discover the motivation to stop your want to give up.

It's necessary to retrain your brain to not crave cigarettes, as we saw in the psychology chapter. This can require a lot of labor. We'll examine some strategies for squelching the need in this chapter.

Make the day you quit a holiday.

First and foremost, schedule a date with yourself. Select a day to give up. A memorable day such as a birthday, anniversary, or real holiday can be used.

Even better, schedule it for tomorrow!

Celebrate your quit day when it arrives!

Notify everyone of your decision to resign. Your pals will be happy for you. Your loved ones will understand this.

Organize a celebration. Telling your buddies you're starting a healthier lifestyle is the best excuse ever to get together and have fun.

Change the pack.

Swapping that pack of cigarettes for a healthier one is a wise first step. Replacing your pack with a picture of a loved one is one method to achieve this. The possibility that you are harming them serves as a strong deterrent to give up.

A pack of gum can also be used as an anti-smoking tool. You grab something else to put in your mouth instead of a cigarette when you reach for it.

Using all the money you will be saving, you may utilize an item that makes you think of something you want to purchase. Maybe a stick to symbolize a trip to the woods. Or a car air freshener for that brand-new vehicle.

Write daily affirmations on index cards and read them each day to help you quit.

Think of uplifting ideas.

A few instances are, "I look better when I don't have a cigarette in my mouth."

"I can complete my work more quickly, easily, or creatively if I don't smoke."

"My friends, family, and neighbours are pleased that I don't smoke."

Write on a few index cards that you have.

Reward yourself.

What does the object you replaced represent? Put your heart's passion into words on paper. Bring it to life.

Place the description in a visible location for daily viewing. Tacked to the TV screen, on your computer, or on the steering wheel of your car.

Calculate how many packs of cigarettes you'll need to purchase your prize using a calculator, then determine how many days it would take to smoke that amount.

After that, you can schedule a time to give it to yourself. Celebrate the anniversary of your resignation. One week and one month following their cessation.

It can take several months or perhaps years if the prize is significant. But think about how much longer you would need to save if you were still a smoker.

Perhaps you might not have been able to get it at all.

Methods of meditation

Meditation is becoming a popular method for life adjustment. It is widely used for anything from depression relief to weight loss.

Changing your mind consciously is a necessary part of the meditation practice. To be able to recognize distractions yet ignore them, you need to become in sync with your body and mind.

Here are some tips to help you get the most out of meditation to help you stop smoking.

Your mind is focused on something when you meditate. That's what we call awareness. It entails accepting your body, ideas, and emotions for what they are right now.

A word, a sound (such as the well-known OM), a phrase, or a mantra can all be used. It's wise to use one of your affirmations.

The secret is to allow every other thought to vanish. Recognize your breathing, but do not attempt to regulate it. Allow your mind to wander as you concentrate on your one concept.

Now, at first, this could be challenging. However, perfection does come with practice. Take ten minutes at a time to try it. You'll be able to extend it to twenty minutes or longer gradually.

The body enters a relaxed condition on its own. You have a serene, tranquil feeling. As you focus on your mantra, you could lose awareness of everything around you, including sound and vision. It'll integrate into your subconscious.

Should you engage in meditation on a regular or even weekly basis, your mantra will eventually become ingrained in your brain. The moment you start thinking about smoking, your mind will falter.

Concentrating on what you are saying or doing is another method to practice mindfulness. Recognize every step of your mental process. Live each day in a way that forces you to focus on what you're doing or who you're with.

You will be able to distract yourself from your craving to smoke in this way. If a craving begins to arise, pause and clear your mind. Next, redirect your attention by using your mantra or sound.

Utilize an affirmation you created previously in this chapter.

When used in conjunction with other smoking cessation techniques, meditation can be quite beneficial.

monitoring hypertension after quitting tobacco

Pressure is a common factor cited by tobacco users as justification for starting again. Both tobacco users and non-users require stress in their lives. As you're stopping, you should acquire more effective techniques for managing stress. For a while, the nicotine trade can be helpful, but in the long run, you'll need other tactics.

As previously said, working is a good way to reduce pressure. It can also help with the fleeting feelings of sadness or misfortune that some people experience when they give up. The executive's workshops and self-help manuals are also under attack. Check out the local bookshop, library, or newspaper.

Otherworldliness might inspire you and help you remember the reasons you must continue abstaining from tobacco. Being indispensable for a choice that might be more important than you is an example of profound practice. This includes, for some, things like church work, petitions, and rigorous practices. For others, it could involve introspection, listening to music, spending time in nature, engaging in creative endeavors, or choosing to assist others.

Think about ways you can control your stress without smoking.

Examine the resources available to you and make a plan for handling the pressures that life will throw at you.

So, How Can It Be Stopped Most Effectively?

Choose a day within the next few weeks, let your loved ones know, and mark the date on your calendar to determine when to stop. Make a strategy to completely give up smoking on that day. Think about the things that might make giving up tough. Make a pre-planned plan for handling any signs of withdrawal. Establish a method to handle or stay away from the items that give you the need to smoke. Get moving before the cutoff point to prevent weight gain after quitting. Locate a constructive distraction to keep your hands and mind busy. Keep nicotine gum and patches handy if you plan to start a nicotine replacement treatment.

It could be prudent to give up abruptly: You can either gradually cut back on your cigarette consumption or carry on as normal before your stop date. Both work quite fine, though it seems like a fast, "cold turkey" stop could be better.

Don't let persistent Inflammation do you any harm: Research has demonstrated that chronic, low-grade Inflammation can worsen type 2 diabetes, cancer, cardiovascular disease, and other conditions. It can also become a silent killer. Discover how to combat Inflammation and maintain your health.

When three out of every five people worldwide die from an inflammatory disease, it raises serious issues.

Fortunately, you have a few options for retaliation: Execute these actions immediately. Fighting Inflammation shows you the way!

Eat first to lessen Inflammation. A number of "anti-inflammatory diets" lack scientific backing, according to Harvard researchers. In addition to important dietary "do's and don'ts," you'll discover the three best diet options in this special study to assist in managing inflammation levels.

Step two: Fighting Inflammation demonstrates how little aerobic exercise is actually required to lower inflammation levels and how doing too much exercise may actually make inflammation inflammation worse. Maintain a healthy weight. Find out the simple techniques that will allow you to concentrate on getting rid of that tummy fat that causes Inflammation.

Getting enough sleep is the fourth step. Getting too little sleep not only depletes your energy and productivity but also exacerbates Inflammation, which is especially dangerous for heart health.

Fifth, sInflammation Experts suggest that inflammatory levels may decline dramatically within a few weeks of stopping. If you've tried to quit before, the strategies in this special report might help you succeed!

Step Six: Cut back on alcohol. Alcohol may either be your friend or your adversary when it comes to Inflammation. Discover why a small amount of alcohol may be advantageous and how much is too much to regulate Inflammation in this special report.

Whether you're attempting to prevenInflammationflammation-related diseases such as dementia, diabetes, cancer, heart disease, or other conditions, the sooner you incorporate these seven measures into your life.

A recent study randomly assigned almost 700 participants to either gradually reduce their smoking over a two-week period or to give up smoking entirely on a prearranged quit date. In addition to alternative short-acting nicotine replacement therapies, both groups received counseling support. At the 4-week and 6-month follow-ups (49% vs. 39%) and 22% vs. 15%, respectively, the group that was instructed to quit cold turkey showed significantly higher rates of successful smoking cessation.

Many people require extra help: While some people succeed on their own, many others struggle, and sometimes it takes multiple attempts before giving up.

Ask for help: Help can be obtained through a variety of channels, such as phone conversations, in-person meetings, and mobile applications. There are several free therapy programs available, and some even give away free nicotine patches.

Apart from your doctor, these are some places to start:

Options for treatment: Pharmacological therapy (e.g., varenicline, bupropion, or nicotine replacement therapy) increases the chance that a patient will effectively quit smoking when combined with counseling. These medications may be used to relieve cravings, withdrawal symptoms, and other undesirable effects of stopping smoking. They can all be used even if the smoker hasn't given up completely. Varenicline and bupropion, which take time to take action, should be started one to several weeks prior to the stop date, depending on the medication. Talk to your doctor about the best course of treatment if you suffer from depression.

If any of these individual therapies don't work, you could potentially try combining them. There are other complementary therapies as well, such as hypnosis and acupuncture. However, it's less certain how beneficial they are.

Take the place of nicotine. Using nicotine replacement increases the rate of cessation. It reduces cravings and the symptoms of withdrawal, and when the withdrawals go away, it's easy to cut back. Several types are available over-the-counter or without a prescription, including nasal spray, inhalers, gum, patches, and lozenges. It is recommended to use the maximum dose patch (21 mg) if the smoker smokes more than ten cigarettes per day. To cease the continuous supply of nicotine through the skin, the patch can be taken off at night. The other short-acting nicotine replacement therapies can be started on a regular basis (e.g., hourly when awake) or used in conjunction with patches when cravings occur.

Varenicline, also known as Chantix. In order to mitigate withdrawal symptoms, varenicline binds to nicotine receptors in the body. This partially activates the receptors without increasing the pleasure of smoking by keeping them from being triggered by nicotine from cigarettes. Varenicline has had the highest rate of cessation in clinical trials so far.

Bupropion, often known as Zyban or Wellbutrin SR. The effect of bupropion is assumed to involve the hormones in the brain. Additionally, it reduces the initial weight gain that comes with stopping smoking. Longer-term care may prevent recurrence in smokers who have quit. It is not suitable for people who have experienced seizures in the past.

The Difficulties of Giving Up Smoking

Giving up smoking is a difficult endeavor. Overcoming the physical and psychological addiction to nicotine takes a great deal of work, motivation, and resolve. While some smokers may be able to give up without any significant problems, for the majority of smokers, quitting is one of the hardest things they have ever done. We will look at some of the main obstacles to stopping smoking in this chapter.

Symptoms of Withdrawal

The withdrawal symptoms that accompany quitting smoking are one of the biggest obstacles. Because nicotine is addictive, quitting smoking will cause the smoker's body to want it. Anger, depression, exhaustion, headaches,

Wants

Another significant obstacle to quitting smoking is cravings. A person may continue to have strong cravings for nicotine even after the acute withdrawal symptoms have passed. There are many other things that can cause these desires, including boredom, stress, and social situations. It can be very difficult to control these desires, and it may take a lot of resolve and strength.

Gain of Weight

Many people worry that if they stop smoking, they'll acquire more weight. This worry is justified because nicotine suppresses appetite, and quitting smoking might cause an increase in hunger. Snacking is also a common substitute for smoking, which can result in weight gain. Controlling weight gain can be a major obstacle for smokers attempting to stop.

Social Coercion

Another obstacle for those attempting to give up smoking is social pressure. Since smoking is frequently a social activity, smokers may experience peer pressure to keep up their smoking. Quitting smoking can also make smokers feel as though they are missing out on social events. It can be challenging to resist social pressure, and quitting smoking may entail finding alternative social activities or having a strong will to stop.

Mental Health Conditions

And last, for those who are struggling with mental health concerns, stopping smoking might be quite difficult. Many who suffer from anxiety, depression, or other mental illnesses turn to smoking as a coping strategy. For some people, quitting smoking can be particularly difficult since they might not have established good coping strategies, which makes quitting smoking much more difficult.

Section Five:

Managing Emergencies

Overview

They are not meant to be used in place of professional assistance, but they may be used in conjunction with therapy or counseling. If you decide to give them a try on your own and feel like you need extra support at any stage, get assistance.

Give Yourself A Small Assistance

Monitoring Drinking Tendencies

It's normal to experience cravings or impulses for alcohol when you adjust your drinking habits. The terms "inclination" and "hankering" refer to a broad range of ideas, real experiences, or emotions that make you want to drink even while you have a slight craving not to. You might detect an odd separation of two titles or a sensation of disarray.

As it occurs, drinking cravings are fleeting, predictable, and under control. Here, we provide a perceived avoidance customized game plan that is commonly used in mental, and social therapy to help people change examples of meaningless reasoning and responses.

With practice and new reactions, your cravings for alcohol will diminish over time, and you'll gain confidence in your ability to control cravings that may still arise occasionally.

If, after two or three weeks, you're still not making progress with the tactics provided, or if you're experiencing really difficult times with your wants, seek the advice of a medical professional. Moreover, several novel, non-propensity frame medications may lessen the need to drink or lessen the cumulative effects of alcohol consumption, making quitting easier.

Identify The Two Types Of "Triggers"

Both external triggers—those in your environment and those within you—can cause an urge to drink.

External triggers include individuals, locations, objects, and times of day that make drinking valuable or educate you about it. Compared to internal triggers, these "dangerous circumstances" are more obvious, predictable, and preventable.

It can be confusing to identify internal triggers because the need to drink almost seems to "spring up." However, if you find yourself questioning whether or not to act on the inclination when it arises, you will discover that it may have been triggered by a fleeting idea, an optimistic inclination such as enthusiasm, a pessimistic inclination such as discontent, or a physical sense such as pressure, headache, or anxiety.

For a few weeks, consider monitoring and evaluating your urge to use alcohol. This will help you become more aware of your cravings—when and how they arise, what triggers them, and strategies for preventing or managing them.

Prevent Dangerous Circumstances

Generally speaking, the ideal course of action is to avoid taking the chance that you'll become motivated, then, at that time, slip and drink. Keep little or no alcohol at home. Avoid social situations when people ask you to drink. If you're feeling embarrassed about declining a welcome, tell yourself that you're not actually saying "for eternity."

In the unlikely event that the cravings subside or become more acceptable, you may decide to gradually ease yourself into a few situations that you currently choose to avoid. Meanwhile, you can maintain relationships with friends by suggesting non-alcoholic optional activities.

Combat Triggers It's Not Possible to Avoid

Since it's impossible to avoid every risky situation or to block internal triggers, you'll need a variety of strategies to deal with drinking motivations.

Here are a few options to consider:

Give a brief explanation of why you are implementing an improvement. Outline your main points on a business card or in an email that you can access easily, such as a notepad section on your phone or a saved email.

Discuss it with someone you can trust. Keep a trusted friend on hand in case of emergency, or bring one with you into hazardous situations.

Take a suitable replacement action to distract yourself. Miss the target, mid-range, and longer decisions—like texting or contacting someone, watching a quick video on the internet, moving heavy objects, taking a shower, pausing, going for a stroll, or spending more time—for different stages of the situation.

Oppose the hypothesis that serves as the inspiration. Put an end to it, examine its flaws, and replace it. Definition: "A single small drink couldn't be harmful. Wait a second, what am I thinking? I've seen 'just one' lead to more parts, so it could hurt. I'm staying true to my decision not to drink.

Take a risk without giving in. Rather than resisting an urge, accept it as a temporary and commonplace place. As bold as you are, keep in mind that it will eventually topple over like a tidal wave.

Evacuate dangerous situations as soon as possible and carefully. It helps you plan ahead for your escape.

The mechanism of action of nicotine

Nicotine serves as an addictive agent. Upon smoking or using nicotine-containing items, nicotine is swiftly assimilated into the bloodstream and expeditiously reaches the brain. Upon entering the brain, heightened concentration alertness and a surge of vigor.

The enjoyable sensation is what entices smokers to continue their habit. Gradually, an individual's body develops a resistance to nicotine, necessitating a higher dosage to achieve the same outcomes. This is the reason why numerous smokers encounter significant challenges in their attempts to quit and have withdrawal symptoms.

Nicotine functions as a brain stimulant and enhances the secretion of glucose, which serves as the primary fuel for the brain. Additionally, it stimulates the secretion of adrenaline, leading to an elevation in heart rate and blood pressure. This leads to the increased heart rate that smokers frequently encounter while smoking.

Nevertheless, nicotine also exerts detrimental effects on the human body. It causes vasoconstriction, which decreases blood circulation and elevates the likelihood of cardiovascular conditions like myocardial infarction and cerebrovascular accident. Furthermore, it exerts detrimental impacts on the respiratory system and heightens the susceptibility to lung cancer and chronic obstructive pulmonary disease (COPD).

Nicotine possesses a high degree of addictiveness, and the cessation of its consumption can lead to the manifestation of significant withdrawal symptoms. The symptoms may encompass irritation, anxiety, impaired concentration, cravings, and sleep disruptions.

To summarise, nicotine is an immensely addictive drug that elicits enjoyable feelings in the brain while also exerting detrimental consequences on the body. Gaining comprehension of the mechanisms by which nicotine operates is a crucial milestone in the process of ceasing smoking and evading its detrimental health ramifications.

thirteen: Conclusion Reflecting on your journey and commemorating your accomplishments. Adopting a more health-conscious and tobacco-free way of living

Section 1: Self-reflection on Your Progress

1.1 Commemorating Your Achievement

Well done! You have reached the end of this ebook, signifying that you have made a substantial stride in enhancing your well-being and adopting a tobacco-free lifestyle. Pause briefly to contemplate your voyage and commemorate your achievements, regardless of their perceived insignificance. Acknowledge the perseverance, tenacity, and dedication you have shown during the process of quitting.

1.2 Recognising the Difficulties

Cessation of smoking is a formidable task, and it is crucial to recognize the obstacles you have encountered throughout the process. Your ability to conquer urges, handle withdrawal symptoms, and navigate challenging circumstances demonstrates your resilience and determination. Take pride in your development, regardless of any setbacks or times of doubt.

Section 2: Adopting a Healthier, Smoke-Free Lifestyle

2.1 Prioritising Your Health and Well-being

By abstaining from smoking, Acknowledge the multitude of advantages associated with adopting a lifestyle free from smoking, including enhanced pulmonary capacity, less susceptibility to various illnesses, heightened levels of vitality, and an extended lifespan. Embrace the beneficial transformations that occur in your physical, mental, and emotional well-being when you quit smoking.

2.2 Expanding upon Your Accomplishments

Cessation of smoking marks the commencement of a fresh phase in one's life rather than its conclusion. Utilize this achievement as a basis for ongoing personal advancement and progress. Utilise the acquired abilities and strategies from this ebook and implement them in various domains of your life. Continue to progress based on your accomplishments and establish fresh objectives that are in harmony with your recently acquired smoke-free way of life.

2.3 Promoting Self-Care and Encouraging Healthy Habits

As you embark on a life free from smoking, make self-care and the cultivation of healthy habits your top priorities. Participate in endeavors that elicit happiness, alleviate stress, and foster overall wellness. Prioritize the maintenance of a well-rounded diet, consistent engagement in physical activity, and ensuring sufficient and restful sleep. Engage in alternative constructive coping strategies, such as pursuing hobbies, cultivating mindfulness, or establishing meaningful connections with cherished others.

2.4 Recognising Potential Obstacles

Although you have effectively ceased smoking, it is crucial to stay vigilant about potential obstacles that may emerge in the future. Remain watchful and acknowledge that the inclination to smoke may sporadically reemerge, particularly during periods of stress or while facing stimuli. Persist in utilizing the tactics and assistance networks you have put in place to manage these difficulties and strengthen your dedication to a life free from smoking.

Conclusion: As you reach the end of this ebook, pause for a moment to acknowledge the advancements you have achieved and the life-altering choice you have made to cease smoking. Contemplate the obstacles you have successfully surmounted and the knowledge you have acquired. Embrace the benefits of your smoke-free lifestyle; keep in mind that giving up smoking is a process, and every day without smoking is a significant accomplishment. Persist in cultivating self-care, establishing beneficial routines, and maintaining awareness of any obstacles. You possess the ability to lead a satisfying life free from smoking, and this undertaking marks the start of a more promising and healthier future.

Commonly Asked Queries.

Is it imperative to cease smoking?

Cessation of smoking is not only imperative but also pressing if you hold yourself and your relationships in high regard.

Does stopping smoking ensure a longer lifespan?

Only God has the power to guarantee someone's survival. Quitting smoking will surely assist in mitigating issues in a society where pollution and disasters exert influence over all aspects of life.

Has smoking had an influence on my family?

It possesses. Members of your family, including your children, are engaging in smoking, which significantly raises their risk of developing numerous health conditions. The cost factor should always be taken into account. It is important to note that when others imitate your behavior, there is a risk that they may adopt the same habit.

Is it possible for me to conquer stress? Is it possible to experience tension even without smoking?

This is all about the preposterous notion that any form of addiction, such as smoking, may potentially alleviate psychological distress. Nicotine just fulfills your cravings. If you want to alleviate tension, stress, or tightness, meditation is a significantly better option.

Will my ability to concentrate be unaffected when I quit smoking?

Cravings for cigarettes are transient and primarily driven by psychological factors rather than the lingering aftertaste, which is only temporary. This is especially true for individuals with a well-established smoking habit. However, the process will just require a few days. Alternatively, you could choose for confections or a dental pick.

Will society maintain its equal acceptance of me?

The current stigma surrounding smoking is at an unprecedented level. Hence, acceptance is not a matter of concern. We believe that you only need to overcome a psychological barrier.

Will the cessation of smoking result in the loss of my elegance?

The practice of bringing a cigarette inside an air-conditioned restaurant is now obsolete. Conversely, there is now a wide array of eateries that prohibit smoking. Due to widespread awareness of the hazards of smoking, smoking is rarely associated with elegance.

Will weight be regained upon cessation?

Affirmative. Nicotine withdrawal will increase hunger.

When it comes to weight loss, there are various options to consider, such as engaging in jogging or performing free hand workouts.

Cessation of smoking can guarantee a reduction in the intake of harmful substances in your everyday existence.

"I had to resume smoking after my initial period of not smoking." Is it advisable for me to make another attempt?

Affirmative. I concur with both options. It is conceivable that recent notable occurrences prompted you to abandon your voluntary limitation, but can you recall to what extent smoking aided you in dealing with that specific stimulus?

The answer may not be affirmative. Therefore, we strongly urge you to make another attempt.

Is it advisable to publicly disclose my planned resignation date?

Studies and research have demonstrated that making a prompt decision to quit smoking has yielded significantly higher success rates. Nevertheless, if an individual holds the belief that revealing a specific date will have a positive impact on their psychological well-being, they may choose to proceed with uncertainty.

Is treatment necessary now that I have relinquished?

The outcome is entirely contingent upon your mental resilience and personal attributes. Some of these have been discussed in the Staying Quit section. Phone therapy is available.

Excessive prudence of the doctor: Cease the act of smoking!

There is substantial data indicating that smoking is detrimental to health. Some individuals, even when they have mild ailments, hardly seek medical attention. They are concerned about the constraints imposed on them by doctors. Why let it be lethal when prevention is more desirable than treatment?

I possess a quite weak cognitive capacity. What strategies may I employ to quit smoking?

Yes. Resigning itself is a commendably courageous decision. The choice also demonstrates your rational thinking, which is rarely exhibited by someone who lacks courage. We recommend that you promptly engage in a conversation with a counselor.

I consume 2 to 3 smokes daily. Does it pose any potential harm?

A snake's initial bite delivers a lethal dose of venom, resulting in a snakebite. The number of external wounds increases significantly after multiple bites.

Is it okay to use a larger filter section on my cigarettes?

The veracity of the aforementioned argument lacks empirical backing from laboratory testing and experiments.

Resignation Smoking poses a significant challenge, but quitting is even more difficult.

We fully agree with you. Although it may provide difficulties, it is possible to successfully reach the summit on one occasion. The challenge lies in persevering despite obstacles. Individuals with impairments can operate automobiles, even in the presence of significant physical limits. The crucial factors are your level of commitment, persistence, and enthusiasm.

Strategies for cultivating the mindset necessary to quit smoking

Creating your smoking habit may prove to be one of the most arduous endeavors you have ever undertaken, but it does not necessarily have to be an agonizing torture for you. If you are determined and follow these four steps, you can successfully overcome your smoking addiction and embark on a significantly healthier of your life.

I will demonstrate the process of altering your mentality in order to permanently quit smoking. Individuals choose to cease their habits for a multitude of motives, including enhancing their well-being, augmenting their financial resources, diminishing their stress levels, and discontinuing negative patterns of behavior. I aim to instruct you on the methods to permanently quit smoking, enabling you to develop a greater appreciation for life beyond your previous experiences. Let us commence!

Cessation of smoking is a formidable endeavor, yet it holds the capacity to be one of the most advantageous actions you can do for your well-being and lifespan, provided that you adopt a suitable method and meticulously strategize. We have consolidated these methodologies, along with additional ones, into an essay specifically crafted to assist you in making a resolute decision to cease smoking. This resource aims to aid you in navigating through this challenging period in your life and ensure that you never reminisce about this habit in the future.

Irrespective of the specific change you desire, altering your habits involves a two-step process. The following steps are as follows: Initially, you must resolve to initiate the desired transformation, and then, you must seek methods to support your efforts in attaining the self-imposed objective. This essay will explore the utilization of these two methods to ultimately eradicate the practice of smoking permanently.

The most challenging component of smoking cessation lies not in the physical act of relinquishing cigarettes but rather in the mental decision-making process and the subsequent unwavering dedication to the chosen course of action. During times of stress, anxiety, or boredom, it is common to fall back into previous patterns, such as smoking, particularly if you struggle with maintaining self-discipline.

Irrespective of the duration of your smoking habit or the level of nicotine dependence, the following guidance can assist you in adopting a determined mindset to quit smoking permanently.

Cessation of smoking can be one of the most challenging endeavors you will ever do, but it is undeniably a pursuit that is highly valuable. Your lungs, finances, and social life will all benefit from this. Below are a few strategies you can employ if you have resolved to quit the habit of smoking cigarettes:

Smokers possess a superior comprehension compared to others that quitting smoking is one of the most arduous obstacles one might encounter. The act of deciding to quit is a crucial milestone; yet, if you lack the determination to carry out that decision, it will hold little significance. Smoking cessation products and hypnotherapy are two approaches that have demonstrated moderate effectiveness. However, neither can be considered a universal remedy. This is particularly accurate when the techniques neglect to consider the particularities of the individual's lifestyle and previous encounters with smoking.

Cessation of smoking is a highly significant and gratifying endeavor that can greatly benefit both your own well-being and the individuals you hold dear. However, it is also an intimidating undertaking if you firmly resolve to undertake it. If you have firmly decided to stop smoking, the subsequent five recommendations will help you feel calm, relaxed, and prepared to shift away from tobacco consumption. You will discover that making the decision to quit smoking is simpler than anticipated. Soon enough, you will eagerly anticipate a healthier lifestyle for yourself and those in your vicinity.

You may have reached a point where you are determined to quit smoking, or you may still be holding onto a small possibility that you may eventually be able to overcome your addiction. Acquiring the knowledge of how to effectively prepare oneself mentally to permanently quit smoking can prove advantageous, regardless of whether one is attempting to quit smoking for the first time, experiencing another unsuccessful endeavor, or aiming to prevent relapse. This guide aims to assist you in altering your perspective on smoking, recognizing the stimuli that prompt you to engage in the act, and honing new strategies to prevent relapse into previous patterns. Additionally, it will assist you in recognizing the stimuli that elicit a positive response from others. Let us commence!

Imagine the significant ease in your life if you were perpetually free from the temptation to smoke a cigarette. Although it may appear unattainable, with the appropriate mindset and diligent application of essential skills, you can actualize that seemingly impossible ambition. This article will provide you with strategies to cultivate a focused and determined mindset, enabling you to successfully overcome your addiction to smoking.

The state of your mental disposition greatly influences your physical well-being and general state of health, including your capacity to overcome the addiction to smoking. Regrettably, smoking possesses such a strong addictive nature that it can lead to the brain being "hardwired" to constantly contemplate smoking, even against one's will. It is feasible to generate novel cerebral pathways, enabling you to cease incessantly contemplating cigarettes. The initial step towards establishing these novel neural connections is to firmly resolve to quit smoking permanently. This tutorial will assist you in achieving precisely that!

Eliminating troublesome behaviors is a complex endeavor, but it is not an insurmountable challenge. Here are several cognitive preparations that can assist you in successfully abstaining from smoking, drinking, consuming unhealthy food, or all three.

Getting Ready to Give Up

Although giving up smoking can be a tough and demanding process, it is a journey that is well worth going on. It's the greatest choice you can make for your general well-being, relationships, and health. This section of the book will teach you how to decide when to stop smoking, get assistance, and get ready to start your path toward quitting.

Set a date for quitting.

A critical first step in your path to stop smoking is deciding on a certain date. It keeps you focused and provides you with a specific goal to strive toward. You can choose a date that holds special meaning for you, like your birthday or the anniversary of the death of a loved one.

Make a plan beforehand.

Plan ahead for your quit date as soon as you've decided on one. Put your quit date on paper and place it in a visible spot so you can see it every day. This will support your motivation and goal-focused persistence.

Establish attainable objectives.

Prior to quitting, make little daily goals that you can work toward. You'll feel accomplished and able to keep on course as a result.

Be in the company of encouraging individuals.

Having friends, family, and loved ones support you in quitting makes it simpler. Tell those closest to you about your plans and solicit their assistance. They are able to support and encourage you during trying times.

Participate in a support group.

Connecting with people who are traveling the same path as you might be facilitated by joining support groups. You may help others, receive guidance, and share your experiences.

Consider using nicotine replacement medication.

Discuss the best solutions for you with your doctor.

Getting Ready to Stop Smoking

Eliminate triggers

Part of your journey is figuring out what prompts you to smoke and eliminating them. This could involve particular hours of the day, pursuits, or pressures.

Establish a wholesome schedule.

A healthy routine can be established to assist in replacing the smoking habit.

This may be learning a new activity, exercising, or practicing meditation.

Be ready for difficulties.

Make sure you are ready by organizing your approach to overcoming these obstacles.

Strategies for Stopping Smoking: The Cold Turkey Approach

Many smokers find it difficult to stop, but it is possible to stop with the correct methods and assistance. Going "cold turkey," or giving up smoking abruptly and without the aid of nicotine replacement medication or other assistance, is a well-liked smoking cessation method. We will go into great length about the cold turkey method in this section of the book, covering its advantages, difficulties, and success strategies.

The Cold Turkey Method: What Is It?

The cold turkey strategy entails abruptly stopping smoking without the use of any additional products or nicotine replacement therapies. The premise behind this approach is that the body will rapidly become accustomed to the absence of nicotine, leading to the eventual resolution of withdrawal symptoms.

Most weekends, I go to bed late in order to deal. I feel as though I've lost a part of myself, my dearest buddy. My entire existence was entwined with smoking. We have spent 35 years together, through good times and bad. Both negative and positive. Warm and chilly. My left-hand feels as though it has been ripped away. It's essential to who I am.

It's awful, in my opinion. I'll die from it. I'll die from it. "I will not smoke today."

When I give up smoking, I'll save $140 a week and save my health. I've saved about forty bucks already. My coughing has decreased. I find it difficult to do anything. Typically, I wake up, smoke, take a shower, and then smoke again.

Monday at nine o'clock

Lauren is at the doctor's with Lauren. She typically smokes when she visits a pharmacy. God, it's difficult. In my bag, you will discover a lighter. You must be occupied. My phone is indeed a boon. I could save my life with this diary. I'm going shopping soon. Usually, there's coffee and smoking. One more difficulty. Alright, sugar-free coffee is fine. It's not too horrible. It is not nice; it tastes like bloody dirt. It's difficult for me to picture myself in circumstances where I would have lit up a cigarette. Every time I face a challenge and overcome it, it gets easier. At work, I even peered into an ashtray. I could have had a little butt. However, I didn't. I'm crying right now. It's incredible. It's really challenging.

It appears that nicotine has left your body after 48 hours. It's currently midday. Anxiety is growing at this point.

Peanut butter-topped crackers for breakfast. It has a horrible flavor. I make an effort to relish the chilly wind on my face. The sun is on my face while I'm cold. A clear blue sky.My grandchildren.My offspring.My partner. I have so much to be grateful for. If you want to smoke, that doesn't help. Now, you're beginning to get a sense of what it's like to be a drug addict. I even experienced sweats, cramping in my stomach, and diarrhea.

I finished cutting my dog's nails in the afternoon and went straight for a cigarette. And I start crying again. What I can do is this. One step at a time, please. Monday at 2:30 pm. I'm heading to the office. One more difficulty. Driving there is insufficient.

11:00 pm.

It was an endless game of will-I or won't-I. I was really craving a cigarette. They have a role in all I do. It seems as though I have nothing exciting in store for me. After finishing something, I would say to myself, "Okay, smoke now." I was able to get assistance from a buddy. This was quite beneficial. My addiction to coffee was another issue. Now, it tastes like muck. It had a muddy flavor. I made multiple attempts to "borrow" a cigarette but ultimately gave up. Hour by hour, it takes place.

4.45 am.

I spent most of the night singing, fantasizing, and picturing, and when I woke up, I had given up smoking. A cup of tea in the cozy living room. I'm feeling optimistic.

Wednesday 8:00 am.

It was training day on Tuesday. I performed fairly well. I must have considered smoking ten times. I promise you that this is wonderful. I spent thirty minutes at the shops. In the rear, in a container, I discovered a half-cigarette. To be honest, I was looking for a lighter to ignite it. I mistook my bag for being in the car. Bill returned. Then he returned. After I arrived home, I spent some time talking to the kids. Felt disoriented.

Had a nap. Slept from 5 pm to 1 am and awoke for roughly sixty minutes. I had a cup of tea in the lounge. I slept from 2 am to 7 am. To be honest, I'm exhausted.

The savings for lunch today came to $100.

It was the fourth day at midday. Work was really demanding today. I was tempted to smoke as I took a seat in the rear. I estimated that while I spoke with my sister, who was here on a visit, I would have smoked five cigarettes. During my office job, I used to say to myself, "I'll go back and have one." I would consider taking a cigarette outside in front. I would reach for a smoke if I had eaten something. If the phone rang, I would light up. Inhale deeply. Continue counting to ten. It's finished. Until the next occasion. Now seated in the lounge. Even if it's frigid outdoors, I think it would still be a good idea to have a cup of coffee and relax in the lounge. Everyone is willing to help.

I've saved $100 as of today, the sixth day. In five more days, the fee will be

$200. I can get my grandchildren a whole swing set. I wish I had more sleep because of this habit. It's a means of escape.

Thursday, June 9.

I've wanted to smoke ten times already today. It helps to breathe deeply. Cravings aren't as strong now. I'm not sure how I'll handle being seated next to a smoker. Although I've been among them, it was simpler for me to remain on the ground.

June 14th, Tuesday

It will be ten days today at noon since I last smoked a cigarette. That means I've saved $200. Those first few days were terrible. Right now, it's simply awful. It's not that bad. I love them so much. I'm now going through a challenging period. I miss some things more than others. For instance, after eating, when I wake up. The final one before turning it in. Halftime in the football match. In the car, returning from work. However, my sleep is significantly improved. It's not the cough. The coughing has subsided. If someone has smoked more than a mile away from me, I can smell it. I have no problem sitting next to a smoker.

June 19, Sunday

However, I remain here and have not taken up smoking. It's been an extremely challenging two weeks. I've had a hard time these past several days. I should smoke, he says. According to him, smoking seven cigarettes a day equals one pack every week. Every three weeks, two smokes a day equate to one pack. It's something I fight against. It goes by fast. I woke up this morning with a full-blown cold. Bloated nose.ache. Additionally, you might wheeze. Feel awful. It wouldn't be bad if I didn't have to smoke. I've returned outside. What I adore is fresh air. Though they are ephemeral, I do occasionally consider smoking. $300 has already been saved. It's incredible. I went to get one just now. I tried to focus on how I felt rather than the good things that happened. secreting mucus through coughing. Breathing problems can be brought on by asthma. The horrible, chronic cough of a long-term smoker.Television advertisements.

Thursday, June 23: I feel like I can go about my life now without having to worry about giving up. I have to say, they continue to be my favorite aspect of my life. Even if you repeat it for thirty-five years, it won't go away. My increased eating concerns me. I have to practice this more. I've gone 20 days without smoking a cigarette at this point. $400 was spared. You can tell when you haven't smoked in a long time. The thing you do is the downside. I want to feel that kick all over again. HOLY MOLY is awful.

www.ingramcontent.com/pod-product-compliance
Lightning Source LLC
Chambersburg PA
CBHW052148110526
44591CB00012B/1895